FLASHCARD   BOOKS

# CLOTHING

ENGLISH

**to**

# FRENCH

FLASHCARD   BOOK

## BLACK & WHITE EDITION

## HOW TO USE:

- READ THE ENGLISH WORD ON THE FIRST PAGE.

- IF YOU KNOW THE TRANSLATION SAY IT OUT LOUD.

- TURN THE PAGE AND SEE IF YOU GOT IT RIGHT.

- IF YOU GUESSED CORRECTLY, WELL DONE!
IF NOT, TRY READING THE WORD USING THE PHONETIC PRONUNCIATION GUIDE.

- NOW TRY THE NEXT PAGE.
THE MORE YOU PRACTICE THE BETTER YOU WILL GET!

## BOOKS IN THIS SERIES:
### ANIMALS
### NUMBERS SHAPES AND COLORS
### HOUSEHOLD ITEMS
### CLOTHES

### ALSO AVAILABLE IN OTHER LANGUAGES INCLUDING:

#### FRENCH, GERMAN, SPANISH, ITALIAN,

#### RUSSIAN, CHINESE, JAPANESE AND MORE.

## WWW.FLASHCARDEBOOKS.COM

# Infant bodysuit

# Le body

**leuh boh-dee**

**Backpack**

# Le sac à dos

**leuh sak-ah-doh**

# Baseball Cap

# La casquette de base-ball

**lah kass-ket-deh-base-ball**

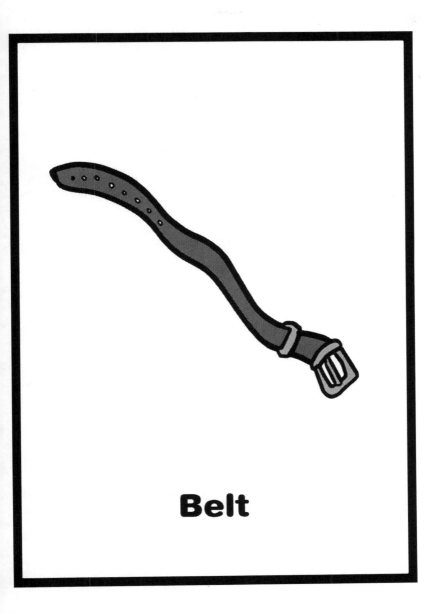

**Belt**

# La ceinture

**lah sah-n-toor**

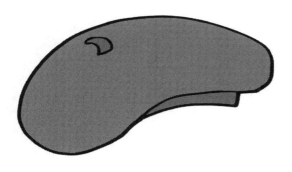

**Beret**

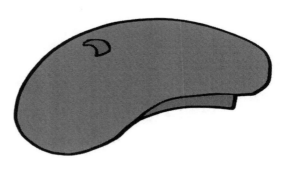

# Le béret

**leuh bay-ray**

**Bib**

# Le bavoir

**leuh bav-war**

# Boots

# Les bottes

**lay boat**

# Bowtie

# Le noeud papillon

**leuh new-ed pap-ee-yon**

# Boxer shorts

# Le caleçon

**leuh kal-sohn**

**Bra**

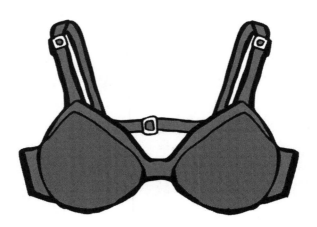

# Le soutien-gorge

**leuh soo-teeyen gor-je**

**Buttons**

# Les boutons

**lay boo-ton**

# Cardigan

# Le cardigan

**leuh car-dee-gan**

# Coat

# Le manteau

**leuh mon-toh**

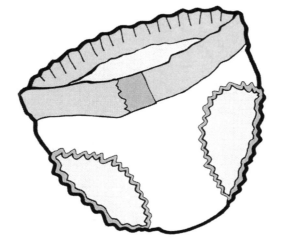

# Diaper

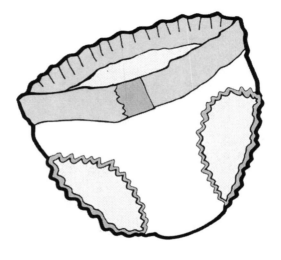

# La couche

**lah koosh**

# Dress

# La robe

### lah roh-bh

# Dungarees

# La salopette

**lah sal-oh-pet**

# Earrings

# Les boucles d'orreilles

### lay book-leh door-ray

**Glasses**

# Les lunettes

**lay loon-net**

**Gloves**

# Les gants

**lay gahn**

# Handbag

# Le sac à main

**leuh sak-ah-muhn**

# Hoodie

# Le sweat

**leuh sweht**

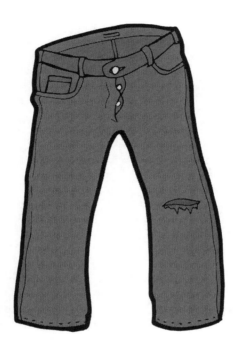

**Jeans**

# Le jean

**leuh jeen**

# Mittens

# Les moufles

**lay moof-leh**

# Necklace

# Le collier

**leuh kol-lee-yay**

**Pajamas**

# Le pyjama

**leuh pee-jah-mah**

**Panties**

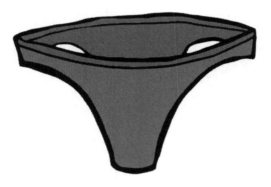

# La culotte

**lah coo-lot**

# Party Hat

# Le chapeau pointu

**leuh sha-poh pwan-too**

# Raincoat

# Le imperméable

**leuh uh-per-may-ahble**

# Ring

# La bague

**lah bag**

# Robe

# Le peignoir

**leuh pay-nwar**

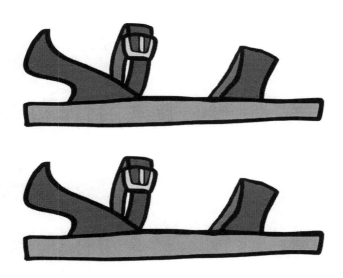

**Sandals**

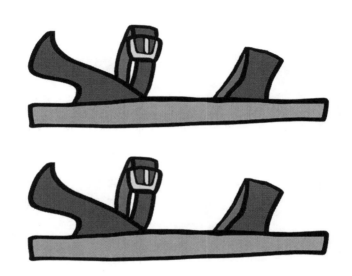

# La sandale

**lah san-daal**

# Scarf

# L'écharpe

**lay-sharp**

**Shirt**

# La chemise

**lah shh-meez**

# Shorts

# Le short

**leuh shorh**

**Skirt**

# La jupe

**lah joop**

# Slippers

# Les chaussons

**lay show-son**

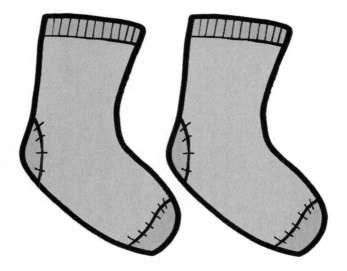

**Socks**

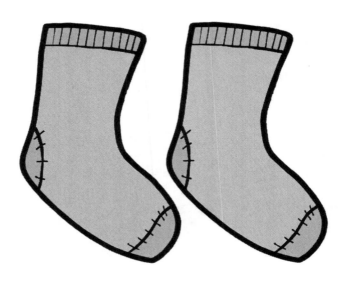

# Les chaussettes

**lay show-set**

# Suit

# Le costume

**leuh koss-toom**

# Sunglasses

# Les lunettes de soleil

**lay loo-net duh so-lay**

# Sweater

# Le pull

**leuh pool**

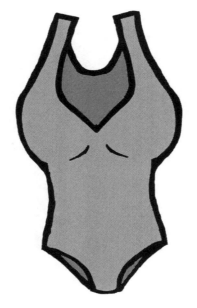

# Bathing Suit

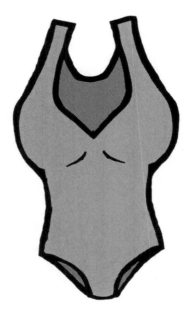

# Le maillot de bain

**leuh my-oh deh buhn**

# Swimming Trunks

# Le short de bain

**leuh short duh buh**

# T-shirt

# Le T-shirt

**leuh tee-shurt**

# Tie

# La cravate

**lah krah-vahte**

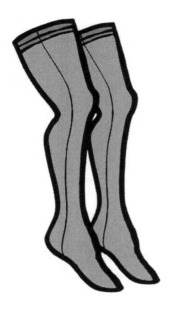

# Tights

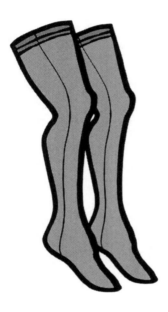

# Les collants

**lay koll-ahnt**

# Top hat

# Le chapeau haut-de-forme

## leuh sha-poh ot-duh-form

# Sneakers

# Les baskets

**lay bas-ket**

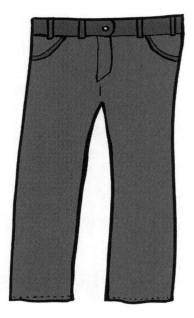

# Trousers

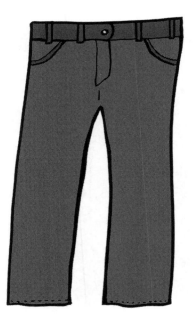

# Le pantalon

**leuh pan-tah-lohn**

# Umbrella

# Le parapluie

**leuh par-ah-plwee**

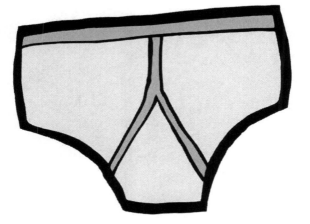

# Underpants

# Le slip

**leuh sleep**

**Vest**

# Le débardeur

**leuh day-bar-dur**

# Waistcoat

# Le gilet

**leuh gee-ay**

# Watch

# La montre

**lah mohn-truh**

# Rain boots

# Les bottes en caoutchouc

### lay boht ohn kah-oot-shoo

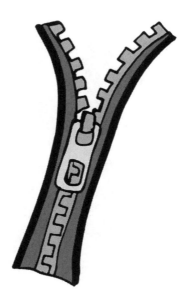

**Zip**

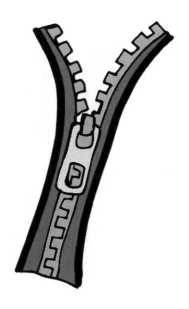

# La fermeture éclair

**lah fair-muh-toor ay-klair**

Made in the USA
Middletown, DE
08 February 2018